Tell Me All About You, Dad

A STUDIO PRESS BOOK

First published in the UK in 2025 by Studio Press,
an imprint of Bonnier Books UK,
5th Floor, HYLO, 105 Bunhill Row, London EC1Y 8LZ

www.bonnierbooks.co.uk

Written by Lucy Dowling
Edited by Georgina Kyriacou
Designed by James King
Cover designed by Maddox Philpot
Production by Giulia Capparelli

Text © Studio Press 2025
Illustrations © Shutterstock

All rights reserved. No part of this publication may be reproduced, stored in a retrieval system, or transmitted by any form or by any means, without the prior permission in writing of the publisher, nor be otherwise circulated in any form of binding or cover over than that which it is published and without a similar condition including this condition being imposed on the subsequent purchaser.

A CIP catalogue record for this book is available from the British Library
Printed and bound in Slovakia

1 3 5 7 9 10 8 6 4 2

ISBN: 978-1-83587-406-6

The authorized representative in the EEA is Bonnier Books Uk (Ireland) Limited.
Registered Office address: Floor 3, Block 3, Miesian Plaza
50–58 Baggot Street Lower,
Dublin 2, D02 Y754, Ireland.

compliance@bonnierbooks.ie

Tell Me All About You, Dad

Written by
Lucy Dowling

Draw a picture of yourself here.

Dad, daddy, da, father ...

If you have been given this book, it means someone special in your life sees you as their father figure and wants to know your story. This is not just a book for a biological parent – it's for anyone who has taken on the role of caring for, and guiding, a child.

From the child's point of view, it can be difficult to see the person behind the parent figure, which is where this book comes in. You are a person who has experienced a full life – someone with dreams and ambitions, with life experience and advice worthy of being passed down.

We hope you can use the prompts and questions within the pages of this book to bring your story to life and create a priceless gift for your child that they can treasure forever.

This book was filled out by…

....

for

....

I would like to tell you my story.

Stick a recent photo of yourself here.

Full name: ....
Age when filling this in: ....
Hair colour: ....
Eye colour: ....
Height: ....
Occupation: ....
Relationship status: ....

I started this book on:

....

Location when filling this in:

....

And I am feeling

....

about filling this in for you.

I hope after you finish reading this, you feel:

....

....

....

The one thing I'd like you to take away from my life story is:

....

....

....

....

Date: .... Signed: ....

Tell Me All About Your Childhood

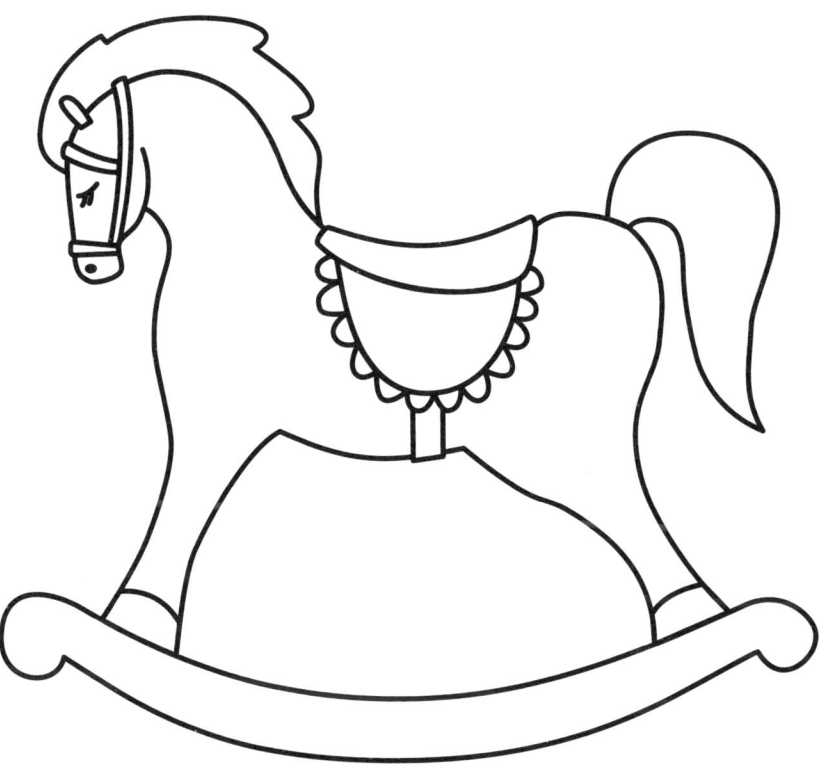

Stick a photo of yourself as a baby here.

Date of birth: ....
Place of birth: ....
Time of birth: ....
Weight at birth: ....
Star Sign: ....
Chinese Zodiac animal:
....
Hair colour: ....
Eye colour: ....

What was the headline news story the day you were born?

Were you named after anybody special?

....

....

Did you have any nicknames when you were little?

....

....

What was your first word? Write it in the speech bubble.

Did you have a favourite teddy or comforter as a baby?

....

Share your earliest memory:

....

....

....

How many homes did you live in growing up?

....

Who did you live with?

....

If you remember it, write your old address or street name below:

....

....

....

What colour was your childhood bedroom?

....

Did you have a garden or outside space to play in?

....

....

Did you have any dens or secret places you would visit?

....

What was the name of the town, village or city that you grew up in? Write it on the signpost.

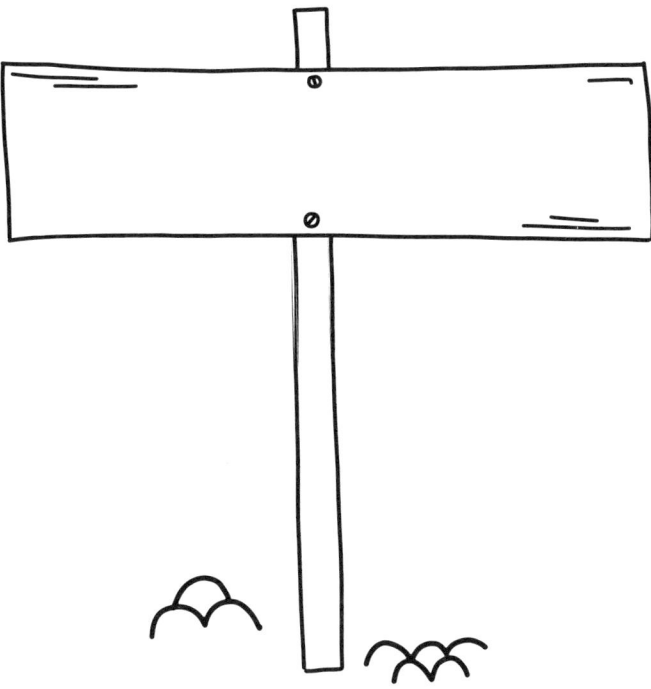

Do you remember any community events?

Do you remember your neighbours? What were they like?

Did you attend nursery or did you have a nanny or a childminder?

....

What was the name of your first school?

....

What did your school uniform look like?
Draw it below.

What were the names of your close friends at primary school?

....

....

What was the name of your favourite teacher?

....

....

Did you enjoy primary school?

....

....

....

What were the most popular playground games?

....

....

....

....

What did you want to be when you grew up?

....

....

Was there someone at your primary school who had a big impact on your life, either positively or negatively?

....

....

....

....

Were you part of any clubs outside of school?

....

Did you collect anything?

....

Did you have a favourite sport? Write it on the T-shirt.

Can you remember three places you visited with your family on holiday?

....

....

Did you grow up in a strict household? What was the most important rule?

....

What was the naughtiest thing you did as a child? Did you ever get caught?

....

....

Were you ever scared of anything?

....

Did you grow out of this fear?

....

Who or what made you feel safe as a child?

....

Who did you look up to when you were a child and why?

....

....

What were your three favourite movies or TV shows?

1. ....

2. ....

3. ....

Who were your three favourite bands or singers?

1. ....

2. ....

3. ....

What was the first music album or single you ever owned?

....

Did you ever attend a music concert?

....

Write the title of your favourite childhood book:

....

What was your favourite dessert to eat?

....

What was your least favourite meal to come home to?

....

What was the best gift you ever received?

....

....

Do you remember any fun weekend routines you and your family had?

....

....

....

....

....

....

Stick some childhood photos of yourself in the frames.

Tell Me All About Your Teenage Years

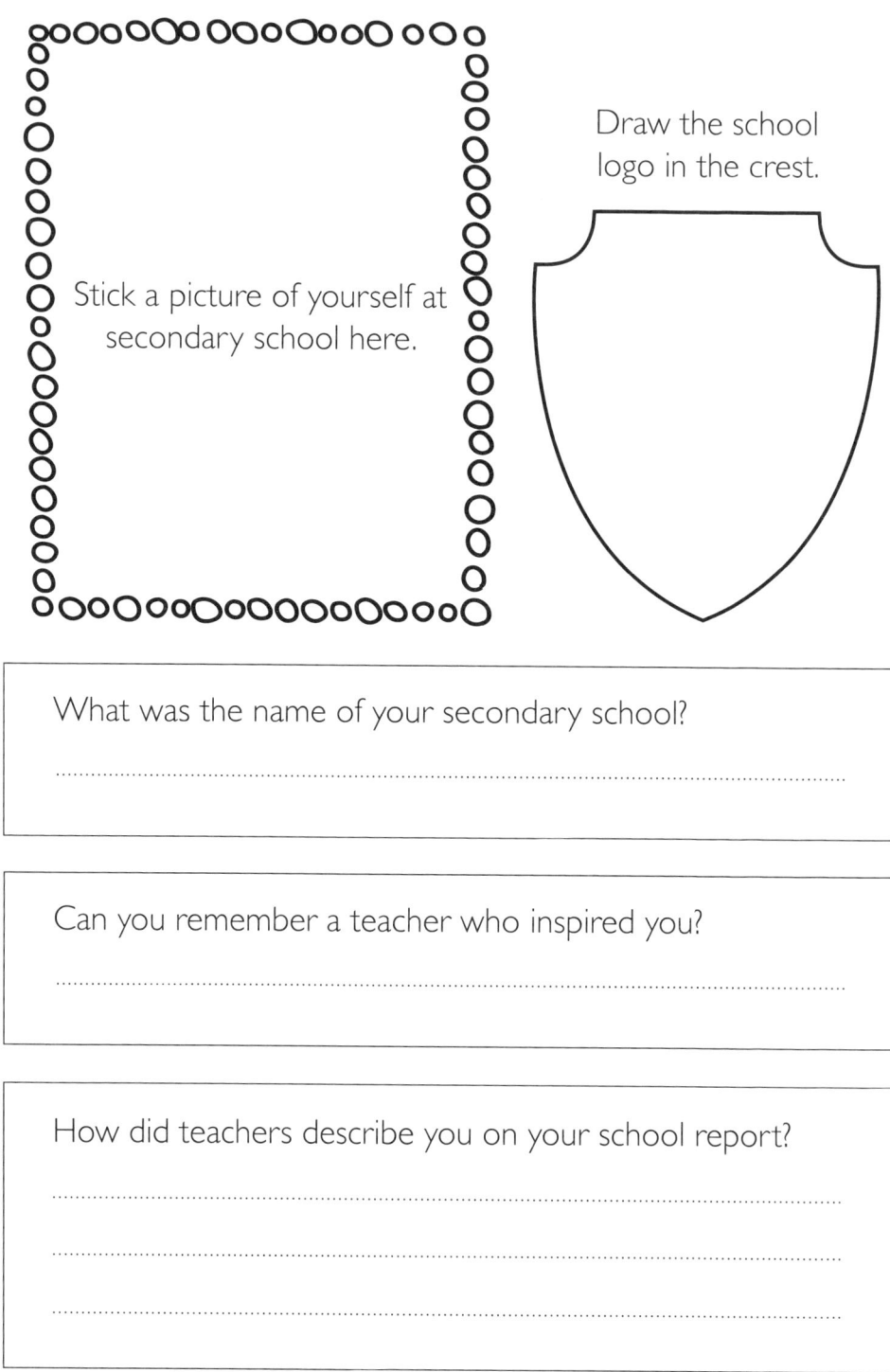

Stick a picture of yourself at secondary school here.

Draw the school logo in the crest.

What was the name of your secondary school?
....

Can you remember a teacher who inspired you?
....

How did teachers describe you on your school report?
....
....
....

Did you ever get detention at secondary school? What did you do?

....

....

What were you favourite and least favourite subjects?

....

....

....

Did you win any awards or prizes?

....

How old were you when you left school?

....

Write any qualifications you received and tell me which was your favourite: ....

....

....

What was the craziest fashion trend of the time?
Did you follow it?

....

....

Draw the hairstyle you had as a teenager on the mannequin head.

Where did you buy your clothes from?

....

....

....

Did you ever get any piercings or tattoos?

....

....

What music did you listen to?

....

What was the must-have gadget of the time?
Did you own it?

....

....

....

Write the name of your favourite sports team on the scarf.

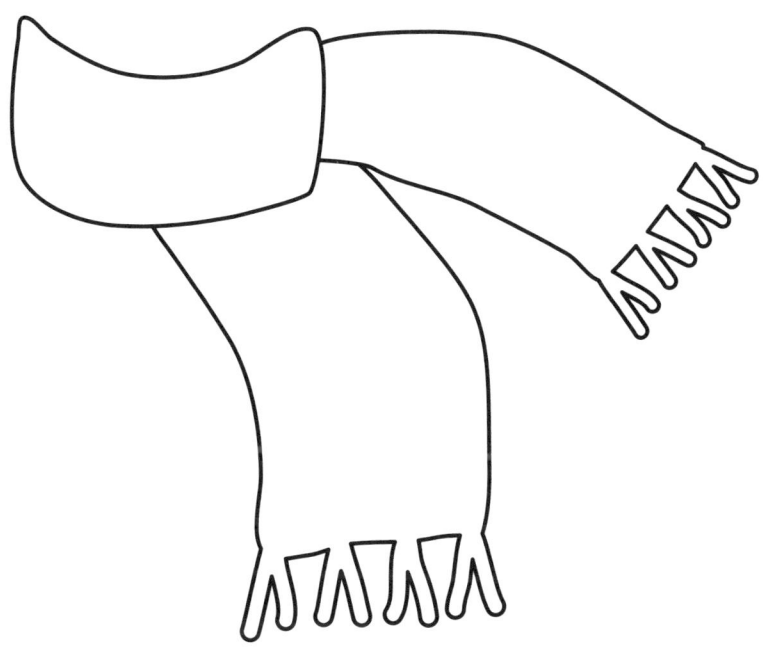

What was the most significant technological advancement during your teenage years?

....

....

Did you get pocket money?
How much did you get?

....

....

Did you have a part-time job?
Write what it was in the name lanyard.

What did you enjoy doing in your spare time?

....

....

Did anyone teach you valuable life skills, such as gardening, budgeting or cooking?

....

....

....

Do you remember the coolest car of the time?
Draw it, or write the name of it below:

....

Was there a car that you dreamt of owning one day?

....

....

If you learned to drive, how old were you when you passed your test? If not, why did you choose not to?

....

....

....

Is there a holiday with your friends or family that stands out as your favourite?

....

....

....

Who was your first date with?

....

How old were you and where did you go?

....

Write how you celebrated your 18th and 21st birthdays in the balloons.

What was the biggest adventure you went on?
....
....
....
....

Did you ever sneak out of the house? Where did you go?
....
....
....

What is the biggest lie you ever told?
....
....
....

Was there a social cause you were passionate about at this time of your life?
....
....
....

Who was your biggest role model?

....

....

....

What was your biggest achievement as a teen?

....

....

....

Tell me something you enjoyed about being a teenager:

....

....

....

....

Tell me something you disliked about being a teenager:

....

....

....

....

If you could go back and give your teenage self one piece of advice, what would it be?

....

....

Is there one thing you know now that you wish you had known when you were younger?

....

....

....

....

What is your biggest regret from this time of your life?

....

....

....

Is there one big life lesson you learned?

....

....

....

Stick some photos of yourself as a teenager in the frames.

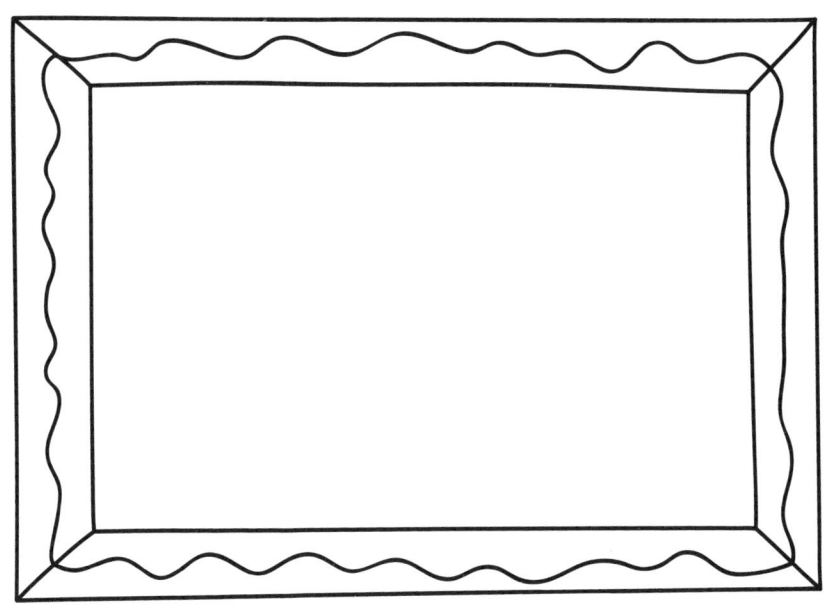

*Tell Me About Your
Journey Through Adulthood*

Stick a picture of yourself in your twenties here.

Did you continue education after you left school?

....

If you did, where did you go and what did you study? If not, which path did you choose instead?

....

....

Did you ever spend time travelling abroad?

....

....

How old were you when you moved out of your childhood home? Write your age on the box.

Who did you live with?

....

Which city or town did you live in?

....

Tell me about a moment where you felt truly independent:

....
....
....
....

Tell me about a time where you found yourself struggling to budget. How did you get through it?

....
....

What was your career ambition as a young adult?

....

What was your first full-time job?

....

What was the biggest challenge you faced early on in your career?

....

What is the best job that you ever had?

....

....

And the worst?

....

....

Did you have a mentor who helped you achieve your career goals?

If you could give me one piece of career advice, what would it be?

Is there something you'd still like to achieve in your professional life?

Looking back, would you have chosen a different career path?

Would you describe yourself as being more of an introvert or an extrovert?

....

....

What did you spend most of your money on?

....

....

Did you have any hobbies to keep fit?

....

....

Did you ever take on any big endurance challenges, such as marathons or hikes?

....

....

Did you ever go to a music festival?

....

What song makes you feel nostalgic about this time of your life?

....

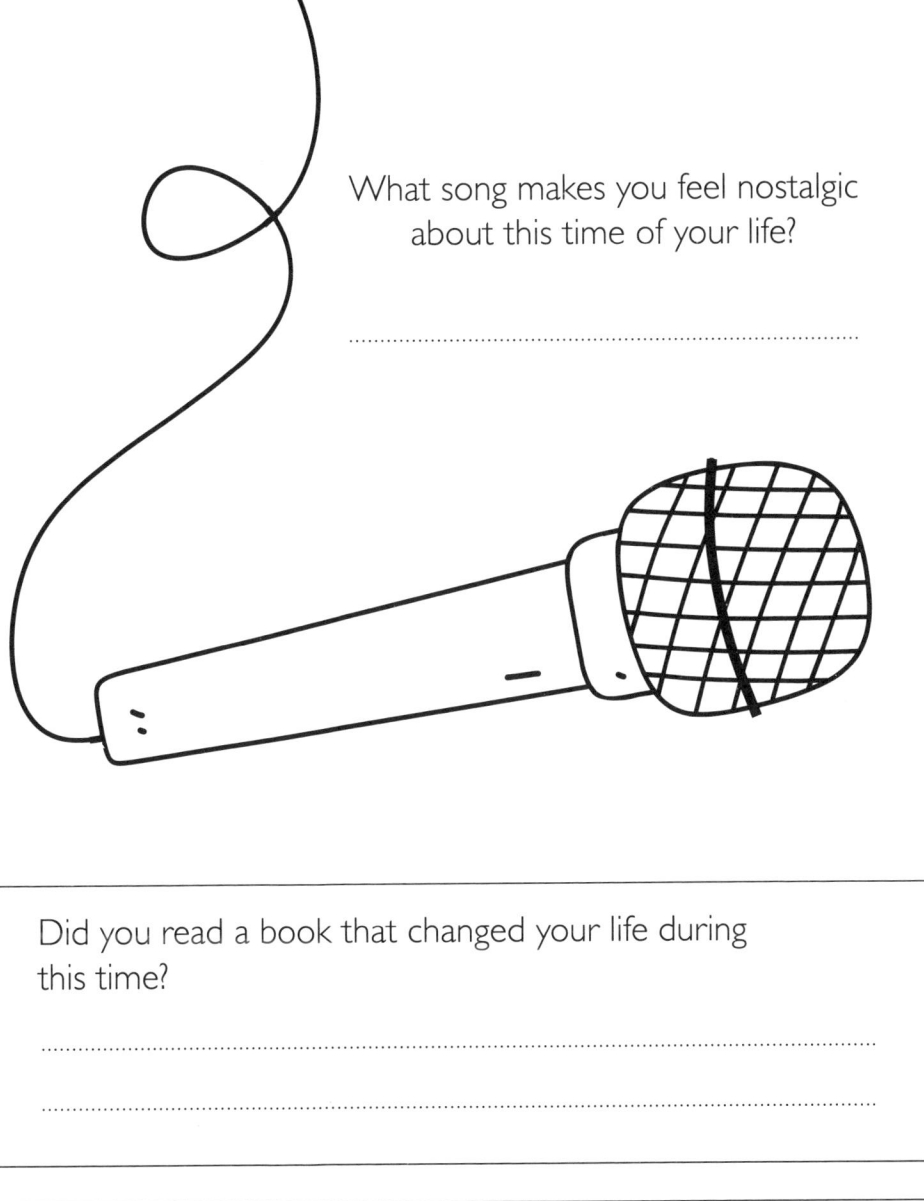

Did you read a book that changed your life during this time?

....

....

Can you remember a world event that had a big impact on your life?

....

....

If there is one thing you could go back and do differently, what would it be?

....

....

....

....

Is there something that you want me to know about you?

....

....

When you look back at your life, is there a memory that still makes you smile today?

....

....

Is there a piece of advice you were given during this time that you will always remember?

....

....

....

....

What was your biggest achievement ...

... in your 20s:

....

....

....

... in your 30s:

....

....

....

... in your 40s:

....

....

....

Tell me about a time during adulthood that was particularly hard for you:

....

....

Who or what helped you get through it?

....

....

Where do you live now, and with who?

....

....

If you're working, what is your occupation?

....

Tell me your biggest achievement to date:

....

What do you value the most in life?

....

Tell me one thing your younger self would be surprised to know about you now:

....

....

Describe yourself in three words:

....

Write three things that are still on your bucket list.

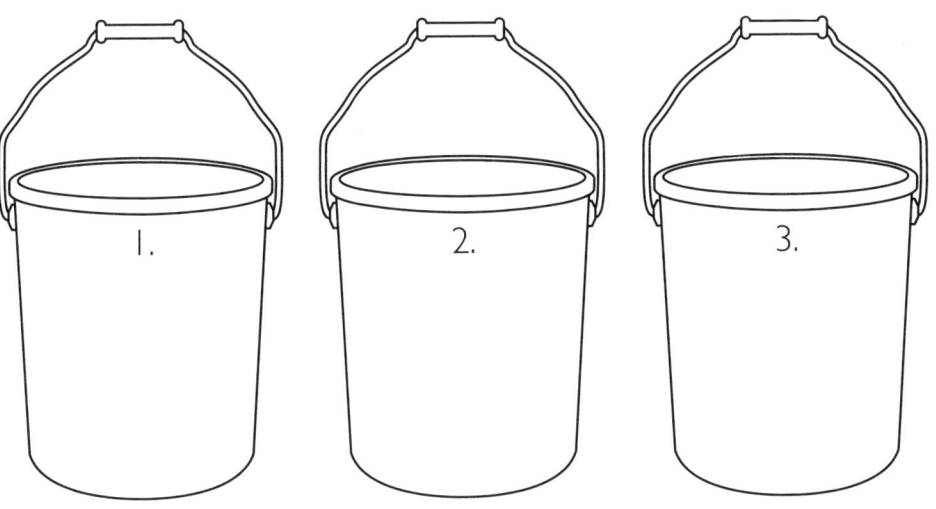

What little things bring you joy? Write them in the stars.

Are you happy?
....
....
....

Tell me your favourite …
- city: ....
- colour: ....
- animal: ....
- drink: ....
- time of the day: ....
- sandwich: ....
- karaoke song: ....
- song to dance to: ....
- song to cry to: ....
- aftershave: ....
- pizza topping: ....

Who would play you in a biopic?

....

What piece of DIY equipment should I always have at home?

....

Tell me your go-to comfort meal when you're unwell:

....

Do you know any cool tricks?

....

....

Tell me a silly joke:

....

....

What is your most prized possession?

....

....

Do you have any phobias?

....

....

If you were stranded on a desert island who would you want to be stranded with?

....

....

Look at the options below and tick your preference.

☐ Health or wealth ☐
☐ Follow your heart or follow your head ☐
☐ Dog or cat ☐
☐ Listen or talk ☐
☐ Teach or learn ☐
☐ Take a risk or play it safe ☐
☐ Books or TV ☐
☐ Sunrise or sunset ☐
☐ Beach or mountains ☐
☐ City life or country living ☐
☐ Shower or bath ☐
☐ Sweet or savoury ☐
☐ Ice cream or ice lolly ☐
☐ Tea or coffee ☐
☐ Minimalism or maximalism ☐
☐ Early riser or night owl ☐
☐ Rock music or electronic music ☐
☐ Globetrotter or home bird ☐

Use a colouring pencil to shade in all the countries that you have visited.

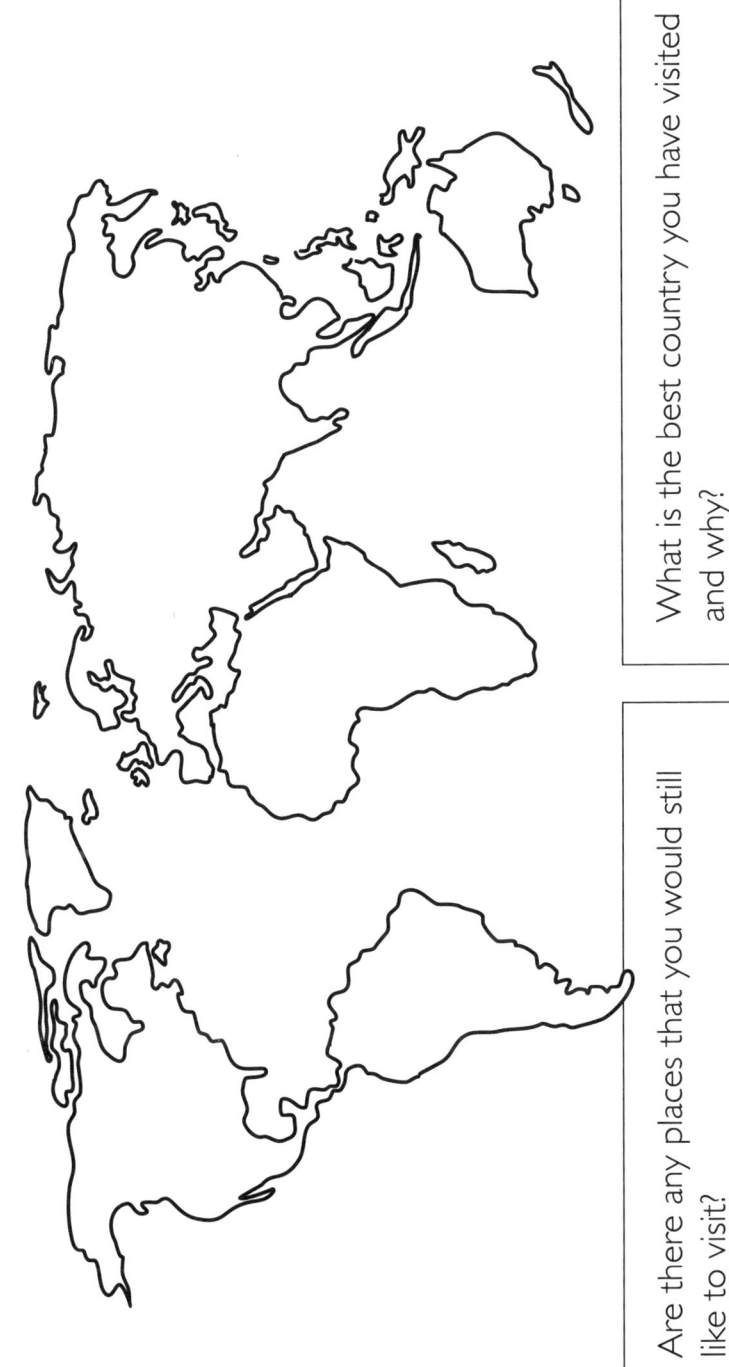

What is the best country you have visited and why?

....
....

Are there any places that you would still like to visit?

....
....

Stick some photos of yourself as an adult in the frames.

Tell Me All About Your Family and Significant Relationships

Fill in your family tree.

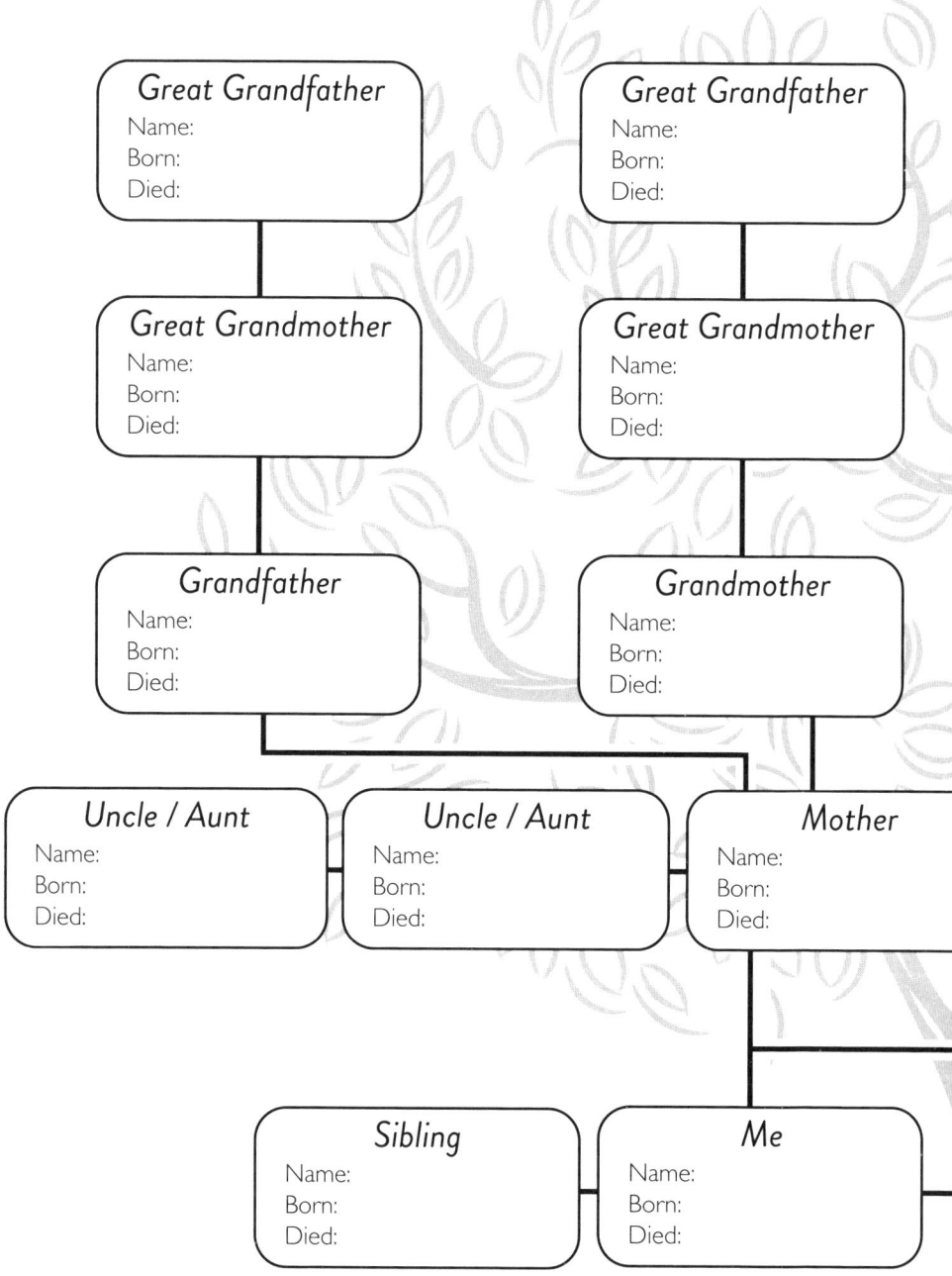

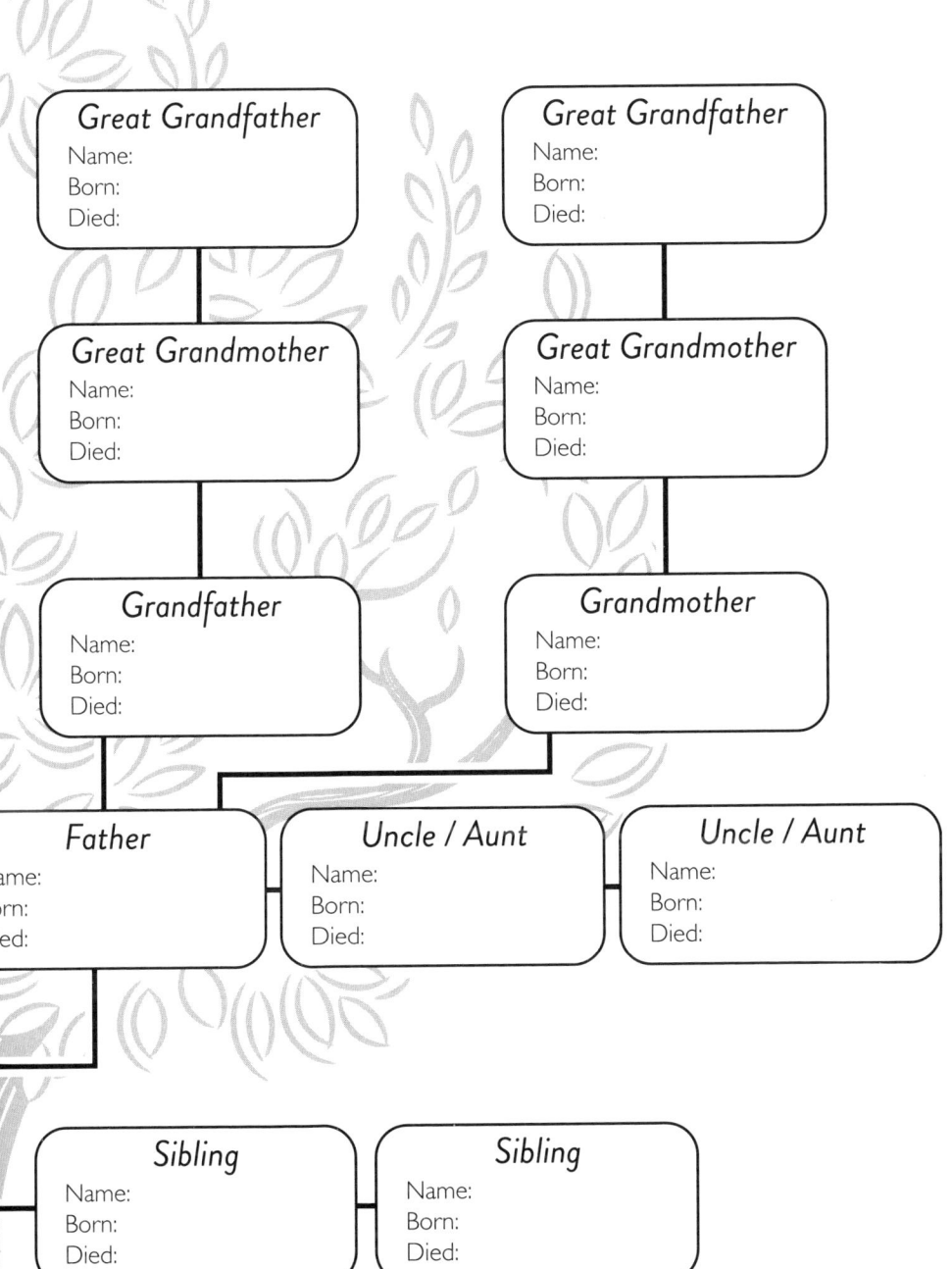

Draw or stick a picture of your mother here.

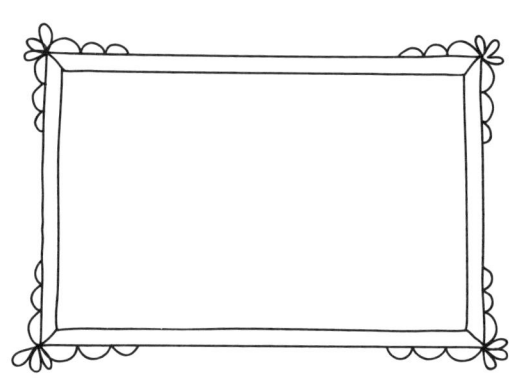

Where was your mother born and where did she grow up?
....

What is the first memory you have of your mother?
....

What smell reminds you of your mother?
....

What similarities do you and your mother share?
....

What was the most important life lesson your mother taught you?
....

Draw or stick a picture of your father here.

Where was your father born and where did he grow up?
....

What is your favourite memory of your father?
....

What similarities do you and your father share?
....

Tell me an important life lesson your father taught you:
....

What is the one thing you want everyone to know about your father?
....

Use this space to write about your siblings or, if you prefer, any cousins or friends you consider as family.

First name: ....
Middle name(s): ....
Surname: ....
Date of birth: ....
Place of birth: ....
Nickname: ....
Eye colour: ....
Hair colour: ....

First name: ....
Middle name(s): ....
Surname: ....
Date of birth: ....
Place of birth: ....
Nickname: ....
Eye colour: ....
Hair colour: ....

How are you and your sibling(s) similar?

....

....

How do you differ from your sibling(s)?

....

....

What do you love most about them?

....

....

Share one or two fond memories you have of your sibling(s) below:

....
....
....
....

Did they ever teach you anything or give you a piece of advice that you would like me to remember?

....
....

Did you ever do something that your sibling(s) got the blame for?

....
....

Are you still close to your sibling(s) now?

....
....
....

Where was your maternal grandfather born and where did he grow up?
....

How old was he when he met your grandmother?
....

Did you get to meet your maternal grandfather?
....
....

Share a fond memory of him here. If you don't have one, share a story you have been told.
....
....
....
....

Write an incredible fact about your maternal grandfather:
....
....
....

Where was your maternal grandmother born and where did she grow up?

....

Did she have any siblings?

....

Did you get to meet your maternal grandmother?

....

....

Share a fond memory of her here. If you don't have one, share a story you have been told.

....

....

....

....

Is your mother more like her father or mother?

....

....

....

Where was your paternal grandfather born and where did he grow up?

....

How old was he when he met your grandmother?

....

Did you get to meet your paternal grandfather?

....

....

Share a fond memory of him here. If you don't have one, share a story you have been told.

....

....

....

....

Is your father more like his mother or his father?

....

....

....

Where was your paternal grandmother born and where did she grow up?

....

Did she have any siblings?

....

Did you get to meet your paternal grandmother?

....

....

Share a fond memory of her here. If you don't have one, share a story you have been told.

....

....

....

....

Write an incredible fact about your paternal grandmother:

....

....

....

Did you and your family do anything special together during the holidays?

....

....

....

Did your family practise a religion and attend a place of worship? If yes, do you still practise this religion today?

....

....

....

Tell me what makes your family unique:

....

....

....

....

Describe the family member who is the most like you:

....

....

....

Describe your best memory from a family gathering or event:

....

....

....

What languages were spoken in your family home?

....

....

Did you have any pets? Write their names and breeds below.

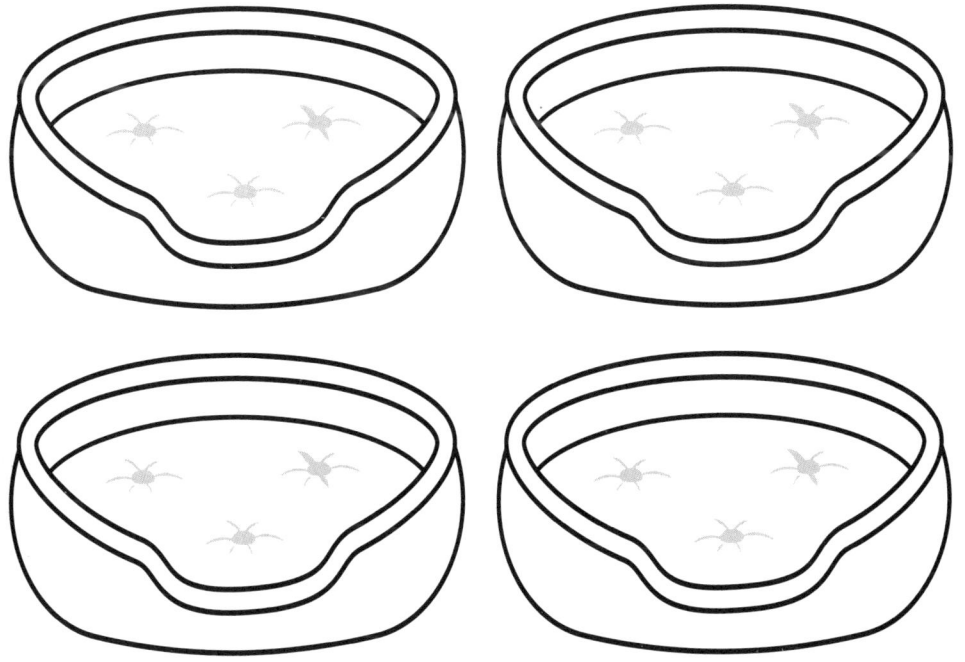

Use the space below to write about a significant friendship you've had that shaped who you are today.

Name: ....

Age you met: ....

Where you met: ....

Are you still friends now?

....

Why was this friendship so special?

....

What has this friendship taught you?

....

....

What reminds you of this friend?

....

What were the names of your best friends at primary school? ....

....

Who was your best friend at secondary school?

....

Tell me about your favourite work colleague:

....

Which of your friends is the most like you?

....

Do you have more or less friends now that you're older?

....

Tell me about a time you let down a friend and how you made amends:

....

....

....

....

Who is your oldest friend?

....

Who is your closest friend now?

....

Tell me all about the love of your life:

- Name: ....
- When did you meet? ....
- Where did you meet? ....
- Are you still in touch? ....
- What did this relationship teach you about yourself and love in general?

  ....

- Why was this relationship so significant?

  ....

- How much of your heart did you give away in this relationship? Shade it in the heart opposite.

Did you ever get married?

....

If you did, when did you know you were ready to propose?

....

Tell me about a time you had your heart broken. How did you move past it?

....

....

What are the most important qualities to look for in a partner?

....

....

What is your best advice for handling arguments in romantic relationships?

....

....

....

....

Use the space below to mention another important romantic relationship.

- Name: ....
- Age you met: ....
- Where you met: ....
- Are you still in touch now? ....

Stick some photos of family members, friends and lovers here.

Tell Me All About You and Me!

Stick one of the earliest photos of us here.

Fill in the fact file about me below:
- Date of birth: ....
- Place of birth: ....
- Time of birth: ....
- Weight at birth: ....

How did you feel when you first saw me?
....
....

Were there other names you thought about calling me?
....

Is there a meaning behind why you gave me my name?
....

Who was the first person you told about me?
....

Can you remember the first thing I said to you?
....

Describe what I was like as a baby in the book.

What was my favourite toy or book? Draw it below.

Tell me your favourite thing that we used to do together:

....

....

....

When were you most proud of me as a child?

....

....

....

Did I say any funny words or phrases?

....

....

....

What is the naughtiest thing I ever did as a child?

....
....
....

Tell me your favourite memory of us from when I was a child:

....
....
....

Do you remember any specific things you taught me?

....
....
....

If you could go back to one part of my childhood and relive it, which part would you choose?

....
....
....

What was I like as a teenager?

Is there a memory of us from my teenage years that still makes you laugh?

Did you ever worry about me when I was this age?

Was there a time you felt disappointed in me?

Did you like my first partner?

What did you really think of my group of friends?

....

....

....

What accomplishment were you most proud of me for?

....

....

What was your favourite way to spend time together?

....

....

....

Tell me about a recent moment together that meant a lot:

Is there something you wish we did more of together?

Is there anything you wish I understood better about you?

Is there something you see in me that I don't see in myself?

What is your biggest hope for my future?

Is there something you want to tell me, but haven't yet found the words?

....
....
....
....

Is there anything I can do to make our relationship stronger?

....
....
....

What is the hardest thing about being my father?

....
....
....

What is one of the best things about being my father?

....
....
....

Stick some recent photos
of you and me together in the frames.

What Do You Want Me to Hold On to?

If you could give me one piece of advice to always remember, what would it be?

....

....

Is there a family tradition you would like me to keep going?

....

....

What song should I listen to when I'm missing you?

....

If you had one wish for me, what would it be? Write it in the shooting star.

Share a memory from our family for me to hold on to:

....

....

What is your best advice if I have a child just like me?

....

....

Are there any family heirlooms you would like me to treasure forever?

....

....

What should I remember when I'm feeling sad or worried?

....

....

....

How would you like to be remembered?

....

....

My Hand Is Yours To Hold

Use the pages below to draw around your hands as they are now. Feel free to sketch in any lines, scars, tattoos or jewellery.

Left Hand

Right Hand

Use the space below to share a family recipe that you would like to pass down.

Dish

Ingredients

Method

A Letter From You to Me

Use this space to write me a letter. It can be as short or as long as you like (feel free to add extra pages of paper). You can use this letter to talk about anything not covered in this book, or anything that is on your mind or in your heart. Something for me to hold on to forever.